<- BRADFORD LIBRARIES ->

B18 681 545 9

CW00766243

H I S

City of Bradford Metropolitan District Council

www.bradford.gov.uk

**Bradford Libraries
Archives & Information Service**

This book is for use in the
library only

METROPOLITAN
BRADFORD LIBRARIES

PRESENTED

THE GRAND TRUNK ROAD

First published in the UK in 2011 by

Dewi Lewis Publishing,
8 Broomfield Road, Heaton Moor
Stockport SK4 4ND
England

www.dewilewispublishing.com

Copyright © 2011

For the oral histories: Irna Qureshi
For the photographs and texts: Tim Smith
For this edition: Dewi Lewis Publishing

ISBN: 978-1-904587-99-6

Design & artwork production: Dewi Lewis Publishing
Print: EBS, Verona

THE GRAND TRUNK ROAD
FROM DELHI TO THE KHYBER PASS

oral histories: Irna Qureshi
photographs & text: Tim Smith

DEWI LEWIS PUBLISHING

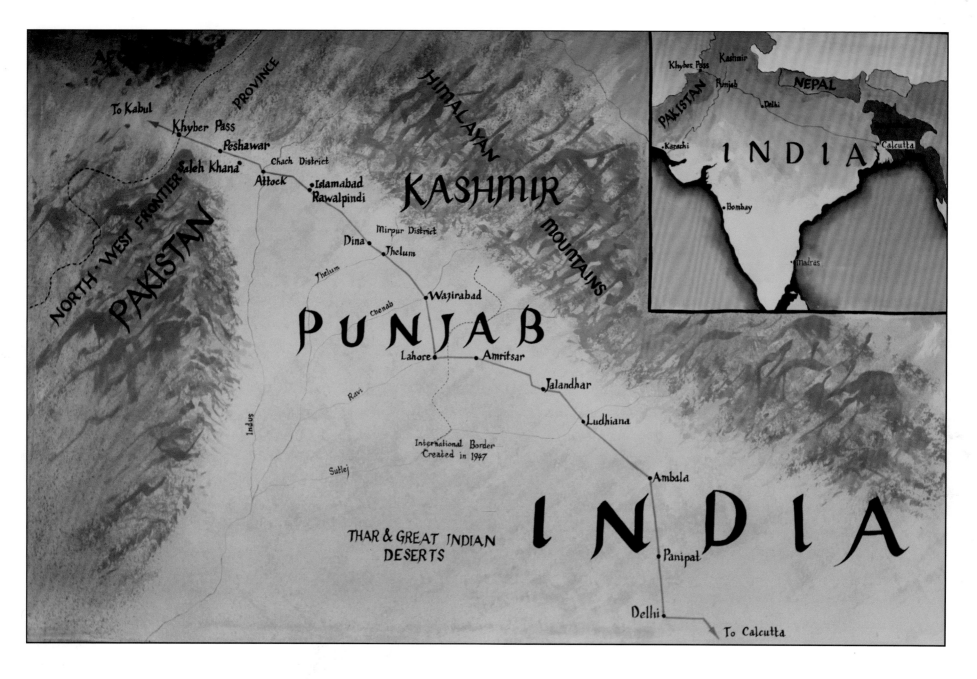

To Kabul

Khyber Pass

Peshawar

Saleh Khana

Chach District

Attock

Islamabad
Rawalpindi

NORTH · WEST FRONTIER PROVINCE

PAKISTAN

KASHMIR

HIMALAYAN MOUNTAINS

Mirpur District

Dina

Jhelum

Jhelum

Chenab

Wazirabad

PUNJAB

Indus

Ravi

Lahore

Amritsar

Jalandhar

Ludhiana

Sutlej

International Border
Created in 1947

Ambala

THAR & GREAT INDIAN
DESERTS

INDIA

Panipat

Delhi

To Calcutta

Khyber Pass

Kashmir

PAKISTAN

Punjab

NEPAL

Delhi

Karachi

INDIA

Calcutta

Bombay

Madras

4

THE GRAND TRUNK ROAD is the oldest, longest, and most famous highway in southern Asia. 1,500 miles in length, it stretches from Kabul in Afghanistan to Calcutta in eastern India. Throughout its history the route has been known by many names. In ancient times it was the Uttarpath or the Great North Route; it then became the Great Royal Road before being renamed the Imperial Road during the days of the Mughal Empire. Officially, the Pakistani section is now part of National Highway 5, and the Indian section is called the Sher Shah Suri Marg, named after the 16th century ruler of northern India who first mapped out the route in its entirety. However, the name that has stuck in all languages is the one given to it by the British: the Grand Trunk Road. Given Indian and Pakistani people's fondness for abbreviations they usually shorten it to the 'GT Road', in fact many know it by no other name.

This book explores the history of the GT Road, showing its importance as a trade and military route. For thousands of years it has shaped the lives of many different ethnic groups, steering the journeys of traders and travellers, conquerors and adventurers. Much has been written on this history but here, for the first time, we explore why the GT Road was so crucial to the process of migration to Britain and how the close links between Britain and many of the places along it continue to this day.

For millennia, those who lived along the GT Road had a much more cosmopolitan outlook than those from more isolated areas of the subcontinent. Contact with travellers and exposure to the ideas and experiences they carried with them broadened the horizons of those living en route. Many travellers would settle along the GT Road on a temporary or permanent basis, and residents themselves used the road to begin journeys that ended in different parts of the world. Large numbers of them came to Britain.

When working amongst British Asian communities, and in the subcontinent itself, we would often hear stories of the GT Road. Looking at a map showing the places from which families had come to Britain made it obvious that the GT Road was important. Alongside Gujarat in India and Sylhet in Bangladesh it defined the area of origin of over 95% of Britain's South Asian communities. The stories of Gujaratis and Sylhetis are well documented elsewhere but the story of the GT Road and its crucial role in migration remained unwritten. It is estimated that, between Delhi and the Khyber Pass, it travels through the homelands of over 90% of British Pakistanis and of the vast majority of British Sikhs and Hindus from the Punjab. The British had ruled the whole subcontinent so why were these areas so well represented in the UK while the vast regions of India and Pakistan were not? The first hand accounts of soldiers and sailors highlighted their pioneering role in laying down the foundations for the mass migrations of the 1950s and 60s. Former soldiers also confirmed that the GT Road was where they joined the army. The fact that the British have never managed to conquer Afghanistan is well known, but from the Khyber Pass the GT Road stretches eastwards all the way to Calcutta. So why, during the days of the British Raj, did recruitment end so abruptly in Delhi? And what was the Road's relevance to sailors? These were some of the questions for which we set out to find answers.

As with travel in much of the subcontinent, a journey along the GT Road is a bewildering mix of the past and the present, rapidly tripping back and forth between the mundane and the momentous. The photographs and stories we gathered on our journeys between Delhi and the Khyber Pass reflect this. Their connecting thread is the profound and continuing impact of the British on the GT Road and its people, and how they in turn have irrevocably altered the fabric of modern day Britain.

My village in the Chach was just off the GT Road, and when I was young and I crossed the GT Road I had this longing to go somewhere. I used to wonder how far this road went, where it ended. You know how it is when you are a child. I couldn't have been more than ten or eleven years old then. There were no buses or trucks in my village, and nobody had a car! But whenever we travelled on the road for a mile or so on a tonga, you would see buses, trucks and cars and I was really attracted by it all. It was like seeing the M1. I wanted to be in that car travelling down this road and I would wonder what was at the other end. All I knew was that this road starts in Peshawar and goes all the way to Bombay – well, that's what I imagined then because people that went to Bombay took this road.

All along the GT Road, people from places like Gujrat, Gujranwala, Mirpur, they have migrated to London, Bradford, Birmingham, Manchester. And I think that they gained some insight into England because of the GT Road and because of the British plying that road. They got some source of livelihood which brought them into interaction with the British and which gave them a sense of connection with England, somewhere that they could go onto and maybe eventually settle. And then they went and gained a livelihood in England, and contacted their cousins and whoever here, who then went over there. So the GT Road became that interconnection that brought these people together, even if they don't realise it themselves. People in northern Chitral or southern Hyderabad have no such affiliation with the British, unlike the people in the cities, towns and villages that pockmark the GT Road.

far left: Businesses on the GT Road in Ludhiana include the English and Desi (homeland) Wine Shop, which is stocked largely with Scottish whisky. Ludhiana is the centre of the textile industry in the Indian Punjab, and a place from which many Sikhs and Hindus have migrated to Britain.
left: Man on a bicycle turns off the GT Road onto a side road near Dina.

HISTORY OF THE GRAND TRUNK ROAD

It is claimed that the GT Road is as old as India itself. The route has been used for thousands of years, although the one on which the current GT Road is based wasn't mapped out until the 16th century. Recent research indicates that places along it, such as Taxila in Pakistani Punjab, have links with both China and the European world of the Greeks that are at least 3,000 years old. It was the Greek leader, Alexander the Great, who 2,300 years ago used the Khyber Pass to cross the mountains of the Hindu Kush and make the region part of his vast empire. Alexander's rule encompassed a vast network of trade and commerce, stretching from the Punjab in the east to northern Africa and central Europe in the west.

The Mughals used the same route when they travelled to India during the 15th century. They were descendents of Mongol invaders who had settled in Central Asia where they had assimilated their far eastern culture with that of the Middle East and Islam. They established their rule of northern India in the early 16th century, forming alliances with Hindu rulers in southern India while allowing Hindus to reach senior positions within their own government or military hierarchies. The Mughals consolidated Islam in the subcontinent and became great patrons of Islamic arts and culture. They bequeathed the region many of its finest buildings, particularly in their great imperial cities of Lahore (Badshahi Mosque), Delhi (Red Fort) and Agra (Taj Mahal), all of which lay on the Grand Trunk Road.

It was Sher Shah Suri, the Afghan founder of the short-lived Suri dynasty which briefly displaced the Mughals as rulers of the region during the 16th century, who established the Grand Trunk Road in its entirety. He planned a route that linked his capital Agra with the remote provinces of his vast empire, a route which is still in use today. Despite more than 450 years having passed, there are still many who consider the establishment of the GT Road as part of their

family's history. Sardar Adnan is a businessman and polo player we interviewed at Lahore Polo Club:

"My original ancestors came with Sher Shah Suri from Persia. He was the king who laid out the original mapping for the Grand Trunk Road. He identified the most suitable track which could be built as a road, one that could bridge the ravines and the rivers and so forth, and that would connect the cities along the way. He laid out the stops every twelve miles so that people could refresh themselves and caravans could take a break or an overnight stay. And wherever these caravans would stop you can still see trees, huge banyan trees for shade, with water and residential facilities.

My family bred horses. They had a thousand horsemen and they would guard the caravans on the GT Road. All the way from Afghanistan through Pakistan they would guarantee their safety. Along the way they would get land where they could accommodate their families and their horses. And they would pledge allegiance to the local king or lord, who would give them a jaghir, a favour of land that rewarded their loyalty. So that was my family's origination to India, they came as defenders of the caravans. Nowadays, when I ply the GT Road I feel like I'm plying history. It doesn't play a daily role in my life but when I'm on the Road I like to reminisce because of our family links with Sher Shah Suri."

Sher Shah Suri died after a brief reign, and his dynasty ended soon afterwards, but the road endured as his outstanding legacy. Some of the features that he established can still be seen, such as caravanserai (highway inns) surrounded by huge banyan trees and water tanks. The planting of trees alongside the roadside was for centuries one of the traditional forms of Indian philanthropy, providing

shade and shelter for resting travellers. The towers that guided Sher Shah Suri's couriers, marking the distance that could be covered by a horse at a full gallop, can still be seen along the GT Road between Delhi and Ambala. When the Mughals re-established their rule, they built on this extraordinarily effective highway of travel and postal communication. The route between the mountains on the Afghan border and the flat plains around Calcutta has changed little since, a stability which can be explained by physical and human factors. The journey avoids deserts and forested plateaus to the south and mountains to the north, as well as areas susceptible to flooding. Sher Shah Suri identified key crossing points on great rivers, such as those still marked by the forts at Attock on the Indus and at Rohtas on the Jhelum. Once fords and ferries were established and fortified for protection (although they have now been replaced by bridges) they have moved little since. The ribbon of human development, the villages, towns and cities that grew up to serve and gain a livelihood from the highway, particularly at points of convergence with other road and river routes, cemented its passage.

It thus became a strategic and commercial artery for all empires that were to follow. At the beginning of the 19th century the Mughals were driven out of the north western areas of their empire by the great Sikh ruler, Maharaja Ranjit Singh. Initially Ranjit Singh's family controlled only the area around Gujranwala, the Punjabi town on the GT Road where he was born in 1780, but the rise of the Sikh Empire was rapid. Their armies pushed the Mughals back to Delhi and the Afghans to the Khyber Pass. In 1802 Ranjit Singh moved his capital from Gujranwala to Lahore, which along with all his military strongholds at Amritsar, Attock and Peshawar, lay on the GT Road. At its height his empire included the Punjab, parts of Kashmir and other Himalayan kingdoms and the region between the Indus River and the mountains along the Afghan border.

During the reign of Ranjit Singh the neighbouring empire of the Mughals disintegrated and control of the region was assumed by the British East India Company (EIC). Since arriving by sea, initially as traders, the EIC had built up formidable private armies and by the early 19th century it was using them to impose British rule throughout the subcontinent. Ranjit Singh maintained a policy of wary friendship with the British, while at the same time building up military forces to deter their aggression. He hired American and European soldiers to train his armies, which incorporated contingents of Hindus and Muslims as well as Sikhs. By the 1830s they were the only formidable force that remained an external threat to the British in India. The Sikh Empire was also India's last remaining independent region not under British influence, but after Ranjit Singh's death in 1839, poor governance and political infighting among his heirs led to its decline.

In 1845 war broke out between the EIC and the Sikhs along the course of the Sutlej River, which marked the border between them. The Sikhs were defeated by the EIC's Bengal Army, made up of soldiers recruited from areas of northern India supplemented with British troops and commanded by British officers. Although Ranjit Singh's youngest son Duleep Singh remained nominally on the throne, his army was reduced to a token force and all major decisions were managed by the EIC. Rebellions against British rule led to the Second Anglo-Sikh War which took place in 1848 and 1849. It resulted in the defeat and total subjugation of the Sikh Empire. The British were able to march their armies up the GT Road to the Khyber Pass. Their authority now extended from the mountains of Afghanistan in the west to Burma in the east.

I can't think of anywhere in the world where one single road has contributed so much. After Sher Shah Suri built the GT Road no one has established any other link between what is now India and Pakistan. All the invaders, except for the British who came by sea, came in through the Khyber Pass. They passed troops along this road, built cantonments and cities along it. The entire industry is on the two sides of GT Road. The road has made an economic contribution, and to the culture, education, and the general awareness of people. You will see a significant difference between the people who are living alongside the GT Road and those who are living deep in the countryside. People along the Road are more cultured, more educated. So you see this road is unique.

left: Calligrapher at work in Lahore. The city is one of the many important centres of education along the road which has acted as a route for the exchange of ideas and learning for thousands of years.

right: Boys flying kites from the ruins of a caravanserai at Gor Khatri in Peshawar. Caravanserai provided food, shelter and secure storage facilities for traders and other travellers. This site has been a significant stopping point for thousands of years, and the remains of important Buddhist, Hindu, Sikh and Muslim buildings are all found here.

left: The GT Road making its way across the vast, flat plains of the Punjab at Taxila. The trees around these modern-day truck stops were planted hundreds of years ago to provide shade around watering places for caravans of camels and horses. above: Gateway of the Rohtas Fort near Dina. This enormous fortification, its outer walls are 3 miles in circumference, was built by Sher Shah Suri as his main base to protect the GT Road in the central Punjab.

My brother was the commanding officer of the Red Fort in 1947 and 1948. The army garrison was in the Red Fort, and I was between [school] terms when my father was transferred to Calcutta. So I was left with my brother and his family and that was an amazing experience you know. That accommodation was built originally for the Mughals, of course. The steps were wide enough and gradual enough for an elephant to climb, and apparently you went into the fort on your elephant. And the rear door opened out exactly at the point where today we have the flag ceremony. And that's where we were living! And so we could open the door and go out onto that little grass mound where the first flag hoisting ceremony of independent India was held. The first time the flag ever went up on free India, we lived one door away from that spot where Nehru stood to hoist the flag. I really wasn't aware of the significance of that moment then. It was a lot of fun and games but I was too young, maybe 12. Looking back now, that's one of the points in time that I would like to go back to, and be outside myself looking on and seeing the crowds outside. I would like to be able to see all that.

left: The Red Fort in Delhi, built as a palace by the Mughal Emperor Shah Jahan between 1638 and 1648. Two major gates were constructed in the walls of the fort to accommodate the Grand Trunk Road: Lahore Gate which faced north towards Lahore, and Delhi Gate which led to the city located on the southern side of the fort.
right: Boys flying kites above the Badshahi Mosque in Lahore. When completed in 1673 it was the largest mosque in the world, and was opposite the Lahore Fort which housed palaces for the Mughal emperors.

The British in India

When the first English ships to reach the subcontinent arrived off the coast of Gujarat in the early 17th century, local seafarers and traders had already been engaged in overseas commerce for nearly 4,000 years. The arrival of Europeans simply expanded a maritime trading network that already included the Middle East, Africa, southeast Asia, Indonesia and China. The English were not the first Europeans to arrive in the Indian Ocean; the Portuguese and the Dutch had already established a lucrative trade with ports in the east during the 16th century. Aware of the profits being made by their competitors, a group of London merchants established the East India Company (EIC) in 1600. They petitioned Queen Elizabeth I, who granted a Royal Charter allowing their company a monopoly of English commerce with 'the East'. The EIC went on to become an extraordinary success, and at its height controlled half the world's trade and earned those who ran it unimaginable fortunes. Its first ships arrived in India in 1608. Over the next 250 years its trading activities – followed by conquest and colonisation – profoundly affected both India and Britain and led to the establishment of the British Raj, the British government rule of India between 1857 and 1947.

The first EIC ships to travel to India simply traded with merchants already there. Many were based in the Gujarati port of Surat which served as the hub of India's maritime trade, gateway to the Mughal capital of Agra and the Mughal's link with the holy city of Mecca. However, the EIC soon decided to explore how to gain its own territorial foothold in the subcontinent, with the official sanction of both England and India. They requested their new King, James I, to organise this and in 1615 he sent the diplomat Sir Thomas Roe to Agra to meet with the Mughal Emperor Jahangir. The EIC sought permission to live and build trading posts in Surat and other areas, and in return they offered to provide the Emperor with goods from Europe. Thomas Roe's *Journal of the mission to the Mogul Empire* records the letter that Jahangir sent to King James offering his full co-operation:

"I have given my general command to all the kingdoms and ports of my dominions to receive all the merchants of the English nation as the subjects of my friend; that in what place soever they choose to live, they may have free liberty without any restraint; and at what port soever they shall arrive, that neither Portugal nor any other shall dare to molest their quiet; and in what city soever they shall have residence, I have commanded all my governors and captains to give them freedom answerable to their own desires; to sell, buy, and to transport into their country at their pleasure. For confirmation of our love and friendship, I desire your Majesty to command your merchants to bring in their ships of all sorts of rarities and rich goods fit for my palace; and that you be pleased to send me your royal letters by every opportunity, that I may rejoice in your health and prosperous affairs; that our friendship may be interchanged and eternal."

The first EIC trading post was built in Surat. By 1647 there were 23 others dotted around the coast of India and more rapidly followed. Bombay's development by the British led to it succeeding Surat as the major port on India's western coast. Along with Madras in the south and Calcutta in the east, Bombay became a major commercial centre from which the EIC ran its affairs, each one guarded by private armies recruited in England. For the first 150 years the EIC's presence was largely confined to the coastal areas. Inland the rule maintained by the Mughal emperors provided a secure framework for trade. Cheap cotton textiles, silks, indigo dye, chemicals and other goods were exported from Bombay, Madras and Calcutta. Vast fortunes were made exporting opium to China, where it was traded for tea prior to the British developing their own tea-growing industry in India.

During the 18th century Anglo-French rivalry in Europe spread to India, and as French trading companies began raising Indian armies the EIC expanded its military activities. It began to recruit local soldiers, commanded by British officers, and imported new cavalry and infantry regiments from Britain who fought the French on Indian soil. As the Mughal Empire went into decline French and British commanders allied themselves with emerging Indian leaders. The EIC moved beyond its role as a trading concern and British influence grew with the signing of power-sharing alliances with local rulers, through devious political rulings and bloody military conquest. As the EIC defeated both its French and Indian enemies, the former governors of commercial settlements became

left: Pakistani soldiers above the Khyber Pass looking over the border with Afghanistan.

leaders of new governments based on the Indian states they had displaced. As the EIC began to function less as a trading concern and more as a nation, there were huge rewards at stake for those who won power. British courts were installed and taxes were collected to finance further EIC trade and maintain its massive armies.

As the birthplace of the Industrial Revolution, Britain itself was undergoing huge changes during the 18th century. The introduction of machine-based production increased the need for both raw materials and the development of markets for finished products at home and abroad. The relationship with India served Britain well in both respects, and an ongoing increase in Britain's wealth also fuelled the demand for goods from overseas. As the 18th century ended a new group of conservatives came to power in London, determined to make Britain the global superpower. To further its interests the EIC reserved for itself a crucial role in the British government's decision-making. Lord Wellesley was an influential voice in London and as the Governor General in India from 1798 to 1805, he held ultimate power there. His new strategy for India, the Forward Policy, did not tolerate any rivals, particularly the French or Muslim regimes resisting EIC rule. Initially the EIC fought Muslim rulers such as Tipu Sultan, who was an ally of the French and killed in 1799, but the British later went on to annex even the most pliant Islamic states. The Forward Policy also stated its intention to impose not only British laws but also western values on India. It also developed an evangelical flavour. Charles Grant, an EIC director, wrote: *"Is it not necessary to conclude that our Asiatic territories were given to us, not merely that we draw a profit from them, but that we might diffuse among their inhabitants, long sunk in darkness, the light of Truth?"*

By the 1830s British India stretched from Burma in the east to the River Sutlej in the west. The river in the Punjab marked the border with the only part of the Indian sub-continent still to fall into British hands, the territories of the Sikh Maharaja Ranjit Singh. After the Sikh ruler's death in 1839 the Anglo-Sikh wars were fought between 1845 and 1849, and the victorious British took over the Sikh Empire and forced his son, Maharaja Duleep Singh, into exile in Britain.

Duleep Singh lived in London, Scotland and at Mulgrave Castle outside Whitby in North Yorkshire before settling at a country estate near Thetford in Norfolk, where he is now buried. Not only did Duleep Singh see his homeland annexed by the British but he also lost his most famous possession to them, the Koh-i-Noor diamond. At one time the world's largest known diamond, it was seized by the EIC and presented to Queen Victoria to celebrate the 250th anniversary of the EIC in 1850. It became part of the British Crown Jewels when Queen Victoria was proclaimed Empress of India in 1877.

The defeat of the Sikhs enabled the British to extend their Empire to the border with Afghanistan. Like previous rulers, the British used the GT Road as the main artery of their settlement and rule of the Punjab and North-West Frontier. They now controlled the GT Road all the way from the Khyber Pass to Calcutta, the first capital of British India and gateway to lucrative trade routes further east. Garrison towns, or cantonments, were built around existing military bases on the GT Road to house armies and civilian officials, and to facilitate the safe and rapid passage of commerce and military force right across northern India. People from the surrounding farming areas came looking for trading opportunities or work. Some used the GT Road to travel to Agra and then onto Bombay, which was the headquarters of the EIC's private navy and the link between India and Britain, and offered many opportunities for work and trade. Many found work on EIC ships and, along with the servants and nannies of British families returning from the subcontinent, small numbers of sailors settled in Britain from the 17th century onwards, becoming the first Indians to live in Britain.

Along the GT Road large numbers of men were recruited as soldiers. The British preferred to recruit men from northern India rather than those from further south, drawn from groups they considered 'warlike' and the 'martial races'. Thus cantonments along the GT Road provided the vast majority of local troops for the British Indian armies. Prior to its conquest of the Punjab, the EIC had relied on troops recruited in Bihar and Bengal to keep control of its territories. These men of the Bengal Army were also used to bring new regions under control and fought as part of the British armies that won victory during the Anglo-Sikh wars.

These wars gave the Sikh and British armies a mutual respect for each other's fighting prowess, and at their conclusion the British recruited large numbers of their former adversaries from the Punjab and North-West Frontier into forces under their command. It was these recruits who went on to fight alongside the British in the most important conflict of 19th century India.

On 10th May 1857 the 'Indian Mutiny' or 'Great Rising' began when troops of the Bengal Army stationed at Meerut near Delhi rebelled against their British officers. These events were sparked off by new cartridges allegedly greased with pig or cow fat, offensive to both Muslim and Hindu soldiers who had to bite the greasy paper coverings off by mouth. When 85 of these soldiers refused to accept these new cartridges they were court-martialled and the majority sentenced to ten years hard labour. The entire garrison at Meerut was made to watch as the men were stripped of their uniforms. The next day the garrison rebelled and freed the imprisoned men, killing any British officers and civilians (including many Indians) who resisted them. When other British forces entered Meerut the following day they found it empty of the rebels who had marched off towards the Red Fort in Delhi, home of the Mughal Emperor Bahadur Shah Zafar. His power had largely disappeared with the disintegration of the Mughal Empire but, nevertheless, the rebels, who were mostly Hindus, sought an alliance with him. As a letter from the rebels' leaders subsequently stated: *"The English are people who overthrow all religions... As the English are the common enemy of both [Hindus and Muslims, we] should unite in their slaughter... By this alone will the lives and faiths of both be saved."* The elderly emperor was elected leader and as the revolt rapidly spread the rebels captured Delhi and other cities. Of the 139,000 sepoys of the Bengal Army all but 7,796 revolted against the British. Supported by a widespread civilian uprising, the insurrection developed into the greatest and bloodiest revolt against a European colonial power during the 19th century.

The underlying causes to this uprising were a reaction to wide ranging and rapid changes engineered by the British. As a legacy of the Forward Policy most economic, political or cultural grievances were ruthlessly dealt with by the British, as demonstrated by events at Meerut. The rebels' leaders consistently argued that they were engaged in a fight against western occupation, and were particularly motivated to defend themselves against the cultural and religious inroads that missionaries and their political and military masters were making in India. To recapture Delhi and restore order elsewhere, the EIC called on troops stationed further north on the GT Road. The Sikhs, Punjabis and Pathans were loath to support the rebels, since they perceived Delhi to be held by an army which had crushed their own independence less than a decade before. Led by their British officers they marched down the GT Road and laid siege to Delhi. It took two years of bloody fighting to isolate and suppress the uprising, and when British forces finally regained Delhi they proceeded to massacre not only the rebel soldiers, but huge numbers of citizens. Those who could escape fled and the former Mughal capital, a sophisticated city of half a million people, was left an empty ruin. Bahadur Shah Zafar was tried for treason by a military commission assembled in Delhi and found guilty of the prosecutor's charge of a "Mahommedan conspiracy" to which "we may mainly attribute the dreadful calamities of 1857." The last Mughal Emperor was exiled to Burma where he died in 1862 and was buried in an unmarked grave.

These events led to a widespread feeling of distrust between the British and Indians, particularly in areas which had rebelled. The Bengal Army was disbanded and from then onwards, soldiers were recruited only from those areas which had remained loyal to the British. The Sikhs, Punjabis and Pathans were still trusted and having proved their worth during the siege of Delhi and other battles, were encouraged to join the army at the cantonments near their homes on the GT Road west of Delhi. Another legacy of the uprising was the decision of the British government to abolish the EIC, transferring all its powers, properties and lands to the Crown. India was ruled by the Viceroy on behalf of the monarch. The British Raj had begun.

left: The GT Road passing the Bala Hisar Fort in Peshawar, built by the Sikhs in 1834 during their rule of what is now northwest Pakistan. The railway, which follows a similar route to the GT Road all the way from Delhi to the Khyber Pass, was added by the British. above: Storeroom at the Punjab War Museum near Ludhiana with mementoes of Sikh members of the pre-independence British and post-independence Indian armies.

Early morning yoga and meditation at the memorial in Delhi erected by the British to commemorate those who lost their lives during the Indian Mutiny.

The grave of John Nicholson in Delhi. He commanded the force of British, Sikh and Pathan soldiers that marched hundreds of miles down the GT Road to lead the battle that restored British control of Delhi in 1857.

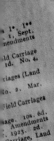

ARTILLERY TRAINING
VOLUME III
WAR
1928

LONDON:
PUBLISHED BY HIS MAJESTY'S STATIONERY OFFICE.

To be purchased directly from H.M. STATIONERY OFFICE at the following addresses: Adastral House, Kingsway, London, W.C.2; 120, George Street, Edinburgh; York Street, Manchester; 1, St. Andrew's Crescent, Cardiff; 15, Donegall Square West, Belfast; or through any Bookseller.

1928

Price 9d. Net.

57-29-0-28.

Muhammad Quraishi

F. A. Class
Islamia College
Lahore.

15.1.25

ON THE OCCASION OF HIS
PASSING THE ENTRANCE
EXAMINATION AT THE UNI-
VERSITY OF THE PANJAB

THIS COPY OF THE NEW
TESTAMENT AND PSALMS IS
PRESENTED BY THE BRITISH
AND FOREIGN BIBLE SOCIETY
TO
Sultan Mohd Khan

FOR HIS CAREFUL READING
AND REVERENT STUDY

ON HIS MAJESTY'S SERVICE.

C.P.D.(M.S.)P.O.W./I/1563.

Issued with the authority of the RED CROSS COMMISSIONER, Simla/Delhi

Dated. 1.10.43.

The following message has just been intercepted from an enemy source.
From: Havaldar Clerk Sultan Mahmud, Ist Indian Ack-Ack. R.

To:- Jahan Dad, village Nila, Distt. Jhelum, R.

"Id greetings to you and the others."

THE SON OF SULTAN MOHAMMAD QURAISHI (SEATED THIRD FROM LEFT IN A PICTURE DATED 1936, WITH COLLEAGUES), REMEMBERS HIS FATHER JOINING THE ARMY.

Everybody joined the army from Chakwal and that's why my father joined. There's nothing but agriculture. There's no irrigation system so you have to hope that it rains often. There was no industry. Neither did people have any technical skill they could offer. That's why it's become a speciality of my area that people joined the army. The British preferred to recruit from this area anyway. I think they saw from experience that Punjabis were loyal and good fighters, nor were they cowards. That's also why they preferred it if your father or grandfather had joined the army before you – they had a better indication of your character.

You had to go to Chakwal because that's as far as the recruiting officer would come to our village. I think there was one recruiting officer for each district, so we came under District Jhelum. I think he was a Britisher because the officers were all British, weren't they! There was a permanent recruiting centre set up there. Other times someone from the local police station would come around and let everyone know they'd be recruiting on such and such date, at whatever time and where it would be happening. This was ongoing recruitment that happened at regular intervals. But if ever they needed extra men then they would make a special announcement. And a gentleman would get out of his car and all the hopefuls would form a line in front of him, and they would be inspected one by one. He would take a man's height into account, and whether or not they had good eyesight, that they didn't have any obvious disability that might stop them being a good soldier. They paid a lot of attention to the caste actually, because I think the British had realised that certain castes made better soldiers than others. So

if he was satisfied he would invite you to the recruitment centre. Then if you were medically fit you were sent off to whichever area to begin your service. Me and my friends were still at school but I remember watching people being recruited like this.

People would wait in anticipation for their sons to grow up so they could join the army. It was considered to be an honour for the family to have a son or two in the army. People would say, "So and so has four sons in the army", meaning he had really come up in the world. If you had four sons in the army, that was four lots of regular income the family was getting. Your son would leave the village and go out to the big city, and he would return wearing the latest shalwar kameez. He would have a towel over his shoulder. He would have a toothbrush. He would start using British soap. All these things he'd probably never laid eyes on until he left the village. He would grow a long moustache. He would put good quality oil in his hair. And he would stand on the street all dressed up and proud for all to see. It was a really big deal.

My father joined the army. He had started college but he had to leave and find a job because he was responsible for a large family. Then my father was sent to Singapore to fight in the Second World War. And then we learnt that he had been captured as a prisoner of war. We got an official letter. First they said he was missing, then we learnt he had been captured. I was given a special privilege because of this; I became exempt from paying school fees. I was about twelve years old. My father was gone for a few years. He returned when the Second World War ended, 1945 I think it was.

Ambassador cars used to transport members of the Civil Service outside the Secretariat Building built by the British in Delhi. Flanking the Rajpath, the ceremonial route from the Viceroy's Palace to the India Gate monument, the buildings now house some of the most important ministries of the Indian Government.

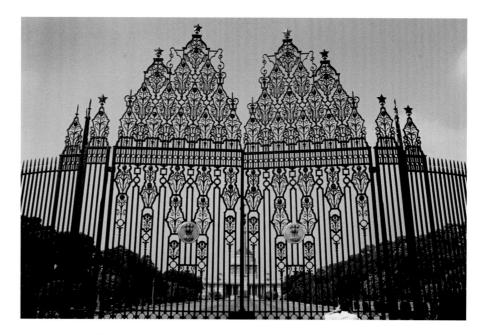

The Rashtrapati Bhavan in Delhi is now the residence of the Prime Minister of India. It was originally built as the home of the British Viceroy.

The importance of the GT Road was critical for the British. The East India Company was here for commerce and this was a major source of wealth for the British Empire, and the GT Road moved what India had to offer. That trade was happening long before the British came here, but they formalised the connection by building a better road. And it moved their military strength and presence which maintained control. Considering the size of the population of India there was no way in hell that the British Army should control India with a handful of officers and men. But their image! And by using their aura they maintained an element of power that was respected. Nobody would mess with them because they looked so good. And the GT Road was their major thoroughfare, all the way from Afghanistan to Burma, it exerted control. And it has not ceded its importance to this day.

The Viceroy of India had more centralised power and more right of authority than the Queen of England. In England she was accountable to a parliament and had to follow some decorum. Here the Viceroy of India was the ultimate power. When the Viceroy of India did his parade along the stretch from Rashtrapati Bhavan to India Gate in Delhi, there would be ten horsemen strong on the right, ten horsemen strong on the left. In front of him would be a carriage of 61 horses and then behind him another 61 horses. Can you imagine that immense show of regalia and power! And the people, the local natives could not look at him. They had to bow down. You didn't look up at the dude, no, that was the law!

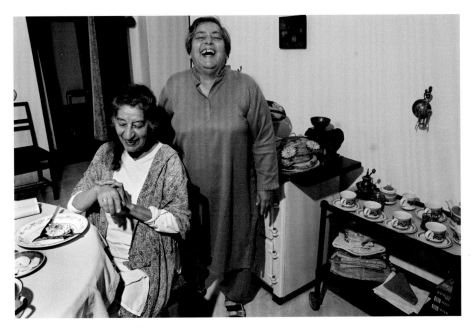

Ratan Bhandari standing next to her cousin Mini Boga at breakfast remembering their childhood when they would be driven up and down the GT Road in a Rolls Royce.

Paramjit Kaur and her son Sandeep Kang outside their home, the former British Officers' Mess in the Jalandhar cantonment. The picture shows her husband's grandfather with King Edward VIII.

Mum tells stories about when Lady Mountbatten gave a party or when they gave a party for Lady Mountbatten. Mum says Lady Mountbatten had a tremendous sense for noticing things. She knew for example that mum loved mangoes, so mangoes were served to Mrs Bhandari. Or that someone else loved cashews and so cashews would be served to that person. And she says that when they gave the return party, the nimboo pani (lemonade) was taken out of enamel buckets with glasses [despite the informality of serving out of a bucket] and put around the table. But Lady Mountbatten is supposed to have taken the glass and sipped the nimboo pani and said how delicious it was. My mum may have attended two parties of Lady Mountbatten. It was something very special if you got an invitation like that. There were a selected few people from certain families who were invited, all members of a certain class. My mum had some very fine saris for parties like that and you chose very special jewellery. You never overdid it, and you had to be on time.

We have had a long association with the British. My [Sandeep's] great grandfather was the ADC to King Edward VIII in 1936. Only four Indian Army officers were selected to go to England to serve with the King, and he was one of them. These officers would ride everywhere with the King, two in front and two behind. They were like the King's personal bodyguards and they were all Sikh. The British liked the Sikhs. They thought they are very honest and very brave, and that is why they were chosen to work with the Royal Family. The Queen was a small girl then. I had pictures of my grandfather holding Margaret and Elizabeth standing next to him, but we had floods and they got ruined. He stayed there for about three years, in Buckingham Palace. This sword was made to order because all four Sikhs were very tall! He was six foot six. When he returned to India, the King gave him a horse to bring back with him.

There is a village in Cherat called Saleh Khana which is very important. Only the old or the women are there in the village, otherwise 90% of them are in England. Saleh Khana people were running the canteens for the army – cooking, making chapatti, curry, selling tea. The [higher] ranks were British of course and the officers would eat in the officers' mess. The troops were actually local Indians and Pakistanis so they would have canteens for them. The Saleh Khana people picked up this profession and they carried it on, so much so that when the Falklands was invaded by the British, the canteen people were from Saleh Khana! And the Saleh Khana people were also in Northern Ireland during the troubled times running canteens for the British troops. And in Cyprus, in all those places where the British troops were. Now they are in England and they are mostly in Birmingham and Dudley because their forefathers were there.

left: Walayat Khan explains how easy it was for him to join the British Army. He walked from his home to a nearby recruiting station in Rawalpindi. He went on to serve in the Second World War and eventually settled in Bradford.

right: Deputy Khan with a photograph of himself and a friend during service in the British Army. The British set up a radio station and army base on the hill above his village, Saleh Khana, and many local men were recruited to run the canteens for the troops.

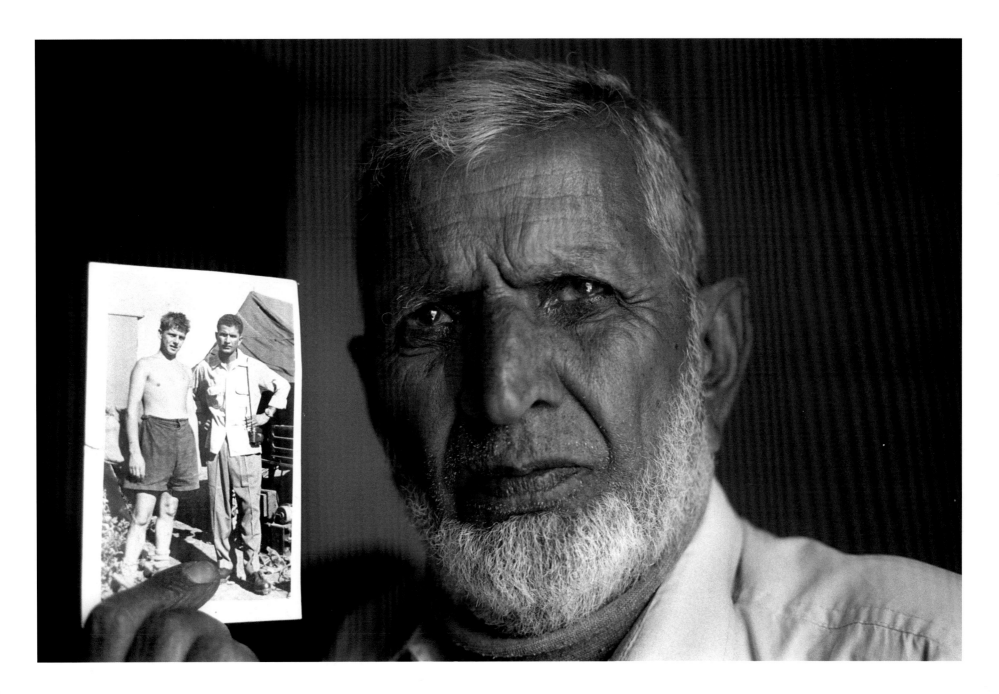

left: Inspection line at the Murree Brewery, the only brewery and distillery in Pakistan. Established at the 19th century hill station of Murree it originally supplied British troops with alcohol. The Parsee owned firm is now based in Rawalpindi and supplies non-Muslims with beer, whisky and other drinks. above: Maintenance work in the whisky vaults at Murree Brewery.

Soldier on duty at the headquarters of the Khyber Rifles in the Khyber Pass. This famous regiment was created by the British and is now part of the Pakistani Army.

Indian soldier on guard duty on the GT Road at the border point between India and Pakistan. The crossing is known as Wagah to the Pakistanis, and Attari to the Indians.

right: Mural in Amritsar showing the massacre at Jallianwala Bagh, a local park where hundreds of people were killed and thousands were injured by British troops in 1919. The face of General Dyer, who gave the order for his soldiers to open fire on a peaceful demonstration, is regularly defaced by visitors to the memorial at the site. The massacre led to Mahatma Gandhi instigating his programme of civil disobedience, and the beginning of the end of British rule in India.

THE PARTITION OF INDIA

1947 signalled the end of the British Raj. Following a nationalist struggle lasting nearly three decades the Partition of India divided the old colonial state into two independent ones: India and Pakistan. Partition was designed to allow the British to withdraw from their Indian responsibilities as quickly as possible. The Indian National Congress, the avowedly secular but primarily Hindu party, headed by Jawaharlal Nehru and Sardar Patel, assumed control of India. The Muslim League, which claimed to represent South Asia's Muslims and was led by Muhammad Ali Jinnah, won Pakistan, the sovereign Muslim state for which it had campaigned. Pakistan became a country of two halves, one half in the east (formerly East Bengal, now Bangladesh) and the other half more than 1,000 miles across India in the west.

The new borders running through the Punjab and Bengal were designed to separate areas with a Muslim majority from areas with a non-Muslim majority. Two commissions were formed to draw up the new borders, each made up of legal experts nominated by Nehru and Jinnah. Both were chaired by the British lawyer, Cyril Radcliffe, who arrived in India for the very first time on 8th July, 1947. When Radciffe met with Nehru, Jinnah and the British Viceroy Lord Mountbatten, he learned that the boundary had to be completed by 15th August. Despite his protests, Nehru, Jinnah and Mountbatten stood firm. The Commission's extremely tight timetable made it impossible to gather the survey and other information vital to a well-informed decision, but speedily provided the political parties with the international boundary that was needed for the transfer of power.

Communities, families and farms were cut in two, and millions of Muslims, Hindus and Sikhs who had shared neighbourhoods for generations suddenly found themselves on the wrong side of hastily drawn borders. Although Pakistan celebrated its independence on the 14th August and India on 15th August 1947, the borders between the two new states were not announced until the 17th August. By delaying the announcement of where these borders ran until after they had handed over power, the British avoided direct responsibility for any repercussions. It was up to the new governments of India and Pakistan to keep public order. In theory no large population movements were contemplated, as plans called for safeguards for minorities on both sides of the new border. This proved an impossible task and there was a complete breakdown of law and order. As many celebrated independence others died in riots and massacres. Over 14 million people left their homes, the majority of them attempting to cross the new frontier that ran between Lahore and Amritsar. Hindus and Sikhs fled to India, and Muslims to Pakistan in the largest migration in human history.

The GT Road, and the railway built alongside it, were the major routes along which these refugees travelled. They were also the scenes of some of the worst violence. In the Punjab alone hundreds of thousands of people were murdered:

The view from the GT Road of the international border between India and Pakistan.

some because of their religion, some for their possessions or land, and others in reprisal for previous killings. Others simply died of hardship and disease along the way. Estimates of the number of deaths vary widely, from several hundred thousand to up to a million people. Vast refugee camps sprang up along the GT Road as people gathered together for protection, or found themselves homeless in a new country. For example, the refugee camp at Kurukshetra near Panipat became home to more than 35,000 people. Delhi received the largest number of refugees for a single city – its population of nearly a million people almost doubled. The refugees were housed in various historical and military locations, such as the Red Fort. On both sides of the border the homeless were eventually found lasting accommodation in newly built houses, in converted buildings and often in the former homes of those who had fled in the opposite direction.

Relations between India and Pakistan have remained tense ever since. At the border crossing (known as Wagah on the Pakistani side and Attari on the Indian side) troops face each other across a heavily fortified border, and the GT Road is now cut in two. Despite a recent thaw in relations it remains very difficult for Indians and Pakistanis to make the journey across the border and vehicles are denied passage. For the time being the GT Road's ancient role as the highway across the subcontinent has come to a halt.

left, above & right: Thousands of spectators gather at dusk every day on specially built grandstands to cheer on each side as the Indian and Pakistani flags are lowered as the border crossing is closed for the night, accompanied by an extraordinary display of military drilling.

left: Hindu woman in Panipat with a portrait of her in-laws who settled in the city after fleeing from Pakistan. above: The ban on vehicles crossing the international border on the GT Road means that all goods have to be transferred between trucks by teams of porters. Indian porters, dressed in blue, transfer a load of tomatoes from a truck in India to their Pakistani counterparts dressed in orange.

TWO BROTHERS NOW LIVING IN PANIPAT IN INDIA SHOW THE HINDU SYMBOLS THEY HAD TATTOOED ON THEIR HANDS TO PROVE THEIR FAITH DURING THE VIOLENCE OF PARTITION. THEIR STORY IS BELOW.

We left Sialkot on the 12 August 1947. It took us 12 hours to reach Lahore and when we got there, people were being massacred left, right and centre at the Lahore Railway Station. Our driver was also a Hindu but he refused to go further until we were certain we were safe. We got to Badami Bagh in Lahore and stopped. We didn't know what to do. Then some soldiers took us to a refugee camp. My uncle refused to leave with us actually. He said, "If I'm going to die, I don't want to do it trapped in a car." We got to the train station and the train wasn't going anywhere. The train driver was a Muslim and he refused to leave for Amritsar without a police escort. Nobody wanted to die. In our hearts of hearts we were thinking, "they'll make an announcement on 15 August and then we'll be able to go back home." We didn't think Partition was really going to happen, and even if it was, we just thought we'll go back and carry on living where we've been living all our lives. We only left Sialkot to get away from the violence. We didn't think to bring anything with us. We just locked the doors and left.

We got to Amritsar on the train in the end. Transport was free. You just got on what-ever mode of transport you could find. Nobody charged you a fare or anything like that. The train came straight to Amritsar from Lahore. There was no question of it stopping anywhere in between. Forget it! You were told to keep the doors and windows closed. From there to Jalandhar on the train. We stayed in a camp they'd set up in the DAV College in Jalandhar, right on the GT Road. We were there just a fortnight. The govern-ment had set up a camp there for the refugees coming from Pakistan. But there were

Muslims travelling up towards Amritsar as well. There we saw some slaughter. One of the Hindu officers had seen his son killed in Gujranwala and he'd now been appointed Deputy Commissioner of Jalandhar. He was inciting people, "Kill them first, and then loot them." Loads of Muslims died in Jalandhar. It stank outside the college, it really did. A body strewn here, another one there. And nobody was interested in picking up the dead either. Everybody was busy running for their own lives. Then Gandhi and Nehru came to Jalandhar to talk sense into the people here. We were only young boys, me and my brother. I remember our elders telling us not to go near the main road because we might get shot or something. Some Hindus got killed by mistake you know. People mistaking them for Muslims because we all dressed the same. We had the 'Om' symbol tattooed on the backs of our hands so people would know we were definitely Hindus. Our elders insisted the whole family have it done.

There were a lot of Muslims in Jalandhar. Even the porters at Jalandhar station were Muslims and they were saying that Jalandhar was going to become part of Pakistan. So that's when we went to Kapurthala. There's more than 300 temples there so that's where the refugees stayed. From there we came to Panipat and we've been here ever since. We were allotted this house in Qalandar Chowk. This had been a Muslim area, you know, but all the Muslims had fled. This place was deserted. There was nobody here except for us. Just like we fled to save our skins I suppose the Muslims did the same.

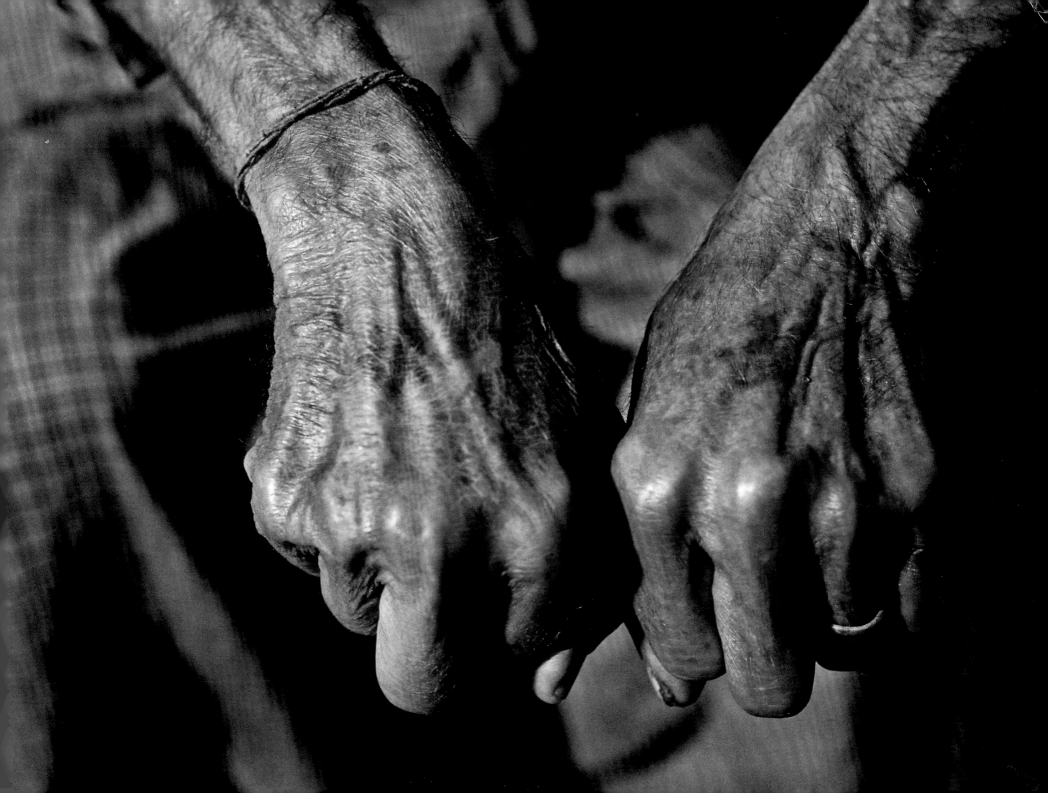

We had a good Hindu community in our village [Nila, District Jhelum]. My school closed when Partition happened because there was nobody to go there. It was a Sikh school. The teachers were Hindu and the students were Hindu and Sikh. Just three of us were Muslim. I had to walk through a big market to get to school and it was run by Hindu businessmen.

I think people started to realise what would happen a couple of years before 1947. Our village was very remote, about 35 or 40 miles from a main city. So it was only the people who had to buy things for their business that went to the big cities, and they must have known that this Partition was going to happen, and so they started to think about disposing their property and everything. And others who didn't know, they just had to carry whatever they could in their hands and leave everything behind.

The people that went to India from our village left their houses and property. Some-body from the government came and sealed the houses so that nobody can go inside. When the Muslim refugees came from India, government needed somewhere to put them as well. So they might have a list – which houses are occupied and which are still empty. Ours was a big village and wealthy too, especially as there were Hindus there and they were business people so they had all the money and everything, and their houses were big houses. So they brought lorry loads of people. I remember they were dropped off in an army truck near our house in the village on the main road, and they were just reading out everybody's name. We were children. We were standing there looking at them sitting there with their belongings – whatever they could carry from their own houses and they were with their children. And the army officer was asking, "How many family members are you?", and then they were handing them the keys of

the empty houses. The people from our village helped them. If a new family arrived, they would go and check that they had everything. If they needed food or anything, they would provide it for a couple of months until they were on their feet. With the houses the army also gave them properties as well, the lands that the Hindus left behind. I think there was a system. They had to show how much land they left behind in their country, so they had to prove that and then they were given the same value of land.

After Partition the schools were full because suddenly so many other people came from India. Ours was the only girl's school so there were new girls every day. Our teacher used to tell us that we have to help these girls. "We are not Indian now, we are Pakistani. You are lucky that you are in this part already, but people in India, they have to come here without anything." Some girls were just in such a terrible situation – no books, no uniforms, nothing. If there were four family members maybe only one was alive who had made it across the border. So the teacher would say if somebody turns up in tatters or very upset or very depressed, we should try to help them instead of laughing at them. We were told that don't tell the girls that you want to help. So we would take our clothes, uniforms, shoes, whatever we could spare, to the office for the staff to distribute. And this continued from 1947 till 1948 and even later because some people didn't leave India immediately. They thought that things will settle down after a while and then we won't have to leave, but then they must have thought that there's no point living in this country because half of the family has gone. Besides, things didn't settle down.

MANY NEIGHBOURHOODS IN INDIA AND PAKISTAN WERE DIVIDED FOREVER DURING
THE 1947 PARTITION. IN THIS STORY, MINOO BHANDARA, A PARSI (ZOROASTRIAN)
BUSINESSMAN WHO WAS THEN JUST A YOUNG BOY, RECALLS WATCHING HIS
NEIGHBOURS FLEEING THE CITY OF LAHORE.

I am a witness to the Partition riots. I was exactly nine years old but old enough to remember certain scenes quite well. You see, we lived on Wallis Road in Lahore which was the upper class Indian locality. The Brits lived in their own areas. I remember Mr Alan, who was the Superintendent of Police who used to live nearby. He was English. His wife was Anglo Indian. All powdered up. His daughter was a girl by the name of Shirley, and his son was Richard. And they were all leaving. They said, "Now we have to go back to our country. We are no longer Pakistani." We didn't have any socialisation with the British. They were a breed apart. So there was no great emotion when they left. We only hoped that their successors, who were Pakistanis, would be as good.

Opposite our house on 21 Wallis Road was a red house, the occupant of which was a Hindu doctor. And father had ordered that all the gates should be barred at all times. And so we used to sneak up to the gate to see through the peepholes what was going on across the road. And I do remember raiders coming to the Hindu house because the Hindus had fled by then. I'm talking of June or July 1947. And they were removing the refrigerator and the furniture and all that. I asked my mother what's going on. And she said, "Well, since the Hindus have fled, the raiders have come over." What we did was – which later in retrospect seemed to be a very dangerous thing to do – we took in a lot of stuff from our Hindu neighbours and kept it at our place. Had the raiders known that a lot of stuff was at our place, then surely they would have come and raided it. So you know all our outhouses – the servant quarters and all – we'd filled them with the belongings of our friends. I remember that very clearly. The garage was full up – cob-

webs and sofa sets. I can remember things coming in but I don't remember the furniture going out. We didn't want to cross the road so we breached the wall so the furniture came in over the wall without attracting too much attention. You see, people left their belongings with us because nobody expected to go for ever. They all thought they would come back and settle back in Lahore when this madness is over.

Another scene I remember is that some of these raiders came in a horse carriage, you know the ones without any top, almost like a Roman chariot. And they came to our gate too. And our cook, Imam Baksh, said, "Well, you know these people are not Hindus. They are Parsis!" So they said, "What are Parsis? What the hell does a Parsi do?" So the cook said, "These are the ancients of Iran." So the raiders said, "Tell them to go back to Iran then! What are they doing over here?" So the cook said, "Alright, I'll tell them to go back to Iran, but can you leave them alone for the time being?" So I think the cook saved us! We were defenceless. Well, we had no weapons anyway!

My parents did not share their agitation with the children but one could feel that they were agitated. They were looking out for security. You see, my father had a number of businesses so suddenly all his accountants, who were Hindus, had left. And my mother who didn't know anything about accounting, he insisted that she become the accountant! And she became the accountant. He probably taught her how to write the books and so on. So that stressed out my mother, suddenly doing strange duties.

Well, of course Lahore was a smaller city, maybe a tenth of today's size. And what I

Derelict Hindu temple in Taxila in Pakistan where the outbuildings are used as homes by local Muslims. At Partition, thousands of religious buildings were abandoned as entire communities fled their homes.

know from the generation that came before me is that Lahore was a very cosmopolitan place. It was very left, socialist, communist, anti-British and all the communities – the Sikh, Hindu, Muslim, Christian – they gelled very well. And they were all involved in progressive movements. It had a very powerful theatre. It had very strong leftist political movements where religious denominations didn't have any meaning. And they were all, of course, anti-British. They all wanted the British thrown out. So in the late 30s, early 40s, Lahore was such a vibrant place. But there was this silence after the Partition. People were stunned by what had happened. And that vibrancy disappeared from Lahore. How could there be any jubilation with all these dead bodies strewn everywhere! I don't recall seeing any jubilation. I can recall people feeling afraid about what had happened and what was to come. Are we safe? Are we not safe? People could not understand how they would physically separate India and Pakistan. I mean, how do you separate this room from the next room? Would they build a canal to separate the two countries? In the end, they put up barbed wire with no man's land in between. But I think up until the 1960s it was still relatively easy to come and go between the two countries and border restrictions weren't as tight as they are today. I remember we used to go to Amritsar frequently to visit friends. I don't recall what sort of permit we had. But they used to visit us in Lahore too.

left: Jama Masjid is Delhi's principle mosque, built by the Mughal Emperor Shah Jahan opposite the Red Fort in 1648. It is still used for worship by the Muslim communities that remain in the city.

above: A single pair of socks are left to dry outside Maharaja Ranjit Singh's tomb in Lahore. The former capital of his Sikh Empire now lies in Pakistan, and the hundreds of rooms once used by travelling pilgrims are empty.

above: Celebrating Basant in Lahore when millions of kites are flown. Originally a Hindu festival celebrating spring it continues as a secular celebration for Muslim Punjabis. right: Applying a mixture of putty and ground glass to kite strings used during Basant. Kite flying in India and Pakistan is a popular and competitive sport where the string is used to cut through that of opponents' kites.

left: Some places of worship which lost their congregations at Partition are now maintained by a skeleton staff, such as this mandir, or Hindu temple, in Peshawar. The rooms for pilgrims on the top floor are unused. above: Graves of members of the British Raj in a neglected cemetery in Delhi.

In 1911 King George V came here [Delhi] for a coronation. Six hundred Indian Princes formed the train. It was the last big spectacle of the age. And Emperor of India he proclaimed himself. My grandfather had got a contract for supplying so many of the things like the horses. So now there are a large number of statues of the British viceroys and kings uprooted and stored there [in Coronation Park] somewhere. I have lodged a movement with a lot of other Indians and we will force the government to make a special museum of them. This is our heritage. The King George V statue was made by this famous Italian sculptor. They are fabulous statues but they are lying in this open park there, some of their noses cut off. It's so stupid! And that statue was originally at India Gate but they moved it maybe 30 years ago. Nehru said, "We'll put Mahatma Gandhi's statue there," but I don't think Mahatma would have liked this kind of thing.

left: The chowkidar, or caretaker, of Coronation Park on the outskirts of Delhi. This neglected park is where the statues of British rulers were moved after Independence, replaced by Indian leaders at prime sites in the city centre.
right: Feral dogs asleep at the foot of the obelisk that marks the spot in Coronation Park where King George V proclaimed himself Emperor of India in 1911.

You see, before anyone becomes a member [of the Gymkhana Club], he is called for an interview. It happens over a cocktail. So they interact with the members and then they vote in a secret ballot – whether they are fit to be members or not. At times we have rejected those people who were multi-multi millionaires for the simple reason that they are not 'clubbable'. We do not consider them worthy of being a club member. It is to do with the way he talks, the way he conducts himself. There are some people who are so rich and they come and start displaying their wealth and connections in a manner that is not acceptable to us.

Polo was originally played by the Mongols and the Persian armies to improve their horsemanship and to learn team building skills, so it was a cavalry manoeuvre. Of all the sports in the world, polo has got it all. You're mastering another animal to play your sport. It has speed. It has thrill. It has hand eye coordination. It has team building. That's why the British regiments adopted it here. The original Prince of Wales, from the Queen Victoria days, took to the sport and then it was taken over to England.

left: Members of the exclusive Delhi Gymkhana Club which was designed and built as part of New Delhi by Sir Edwin Lutyens when the city became the new capital of British India in 1911.
right: Pakistani army officers discuss tactics during a polo tournament at Rawalpindi Polo Club.

AYAHS AND SERVANTS ARE NOT ALLOWED IN THE KASHMIR LAWN AND SWIMMING POOL AREA THEY ARE ONLY ALLOWED IN THE CHILDREN'S PARK

The Christian community is spread out throughout Pakistan. We have equal numbers of Protestants and Catholics in Pakistan. We have thousands of churches. I mean, just look at Jhelum. It's such a small little place but even here we have six churches. Basically, we're all military people around Jhelum. I'm a military chaplain myself. You have to join the military if you want to run this church. For every household in Jhelum, there are at least five people who have joined the military. There is nothing else to do here. No crops! There is nowhere round here to grow anything. No land – it's all pebbles and you can't grow anything on that. So people thought, "Well, at least if we join the military, we will earn something and that will keep us going." That's probably why people from this area have gone abroad as well. There's no industry, there's nothing here.

left: Padari Akbar, the Military Chaplin in Jhelum, outside his church which was once at the centre of an important British cantonment. It now serves Pakistani Christians.
right: Drinking tea after the Sunday service at Lahore Cathedral.

The Shiraz Brass Band relaxing at their office in Peshawar. One of scores of such bands in the city, their European instruments are a legacy of the military and school bands originally set up by the British.

Many of the brass and marching bands still wear uniforms based on British military uniforms. This band clad in Scottish tartans is playing at a Sikh wedding held in a garden on the GT Road near Jalandhar.

right: Students at Edwardes College. Originally a missionary school established by the British Commissioner of Peshawar, it is now a thriving co-educational school.

Migration to Britain

The census figures of 2001 indicate that there are over two million people in Britain who can trace their origins back to India, Pakistan and Bangladesh. But Britain's South Asians are not representative of the entire subcontinent since they originate from a small number of specific areas, largely determined by the origins of the pioneers who came to Britain before the mass migrations that began in the early 1950s. Over 95% of them fall into one of three broad groups: those from the coastal regions in the Indian state of Gujarat just north of Bombay; those from the district of Sylhet in northeastern Bangladesh; and those from towns and villages along the GT Road between Delhi and the Khyber Pass. This book is about the third group, but there are related reasons why so many migrants have come to Britain from these three specific areas. Gujarat, Sylhet and the Punjab/North West Frontier region are far apart and very different from each other. What they do share, however, are the stories of soldiers and sailors and the sea, and the role each played in the days of the British Empire.

Gujarat was Britain's first point of contact with India when ships sailing from London arrived at the port of Surat in 1608. When Bombay subsequently developed as the maritime city that linked India and Britain it was the British that ruled it, but it was Gujarati businessmen, traders and workers that ran it. Their role was important not only in Asia. Gujarati traders were already active in most of East Africa's coastal cities when Britain led the European charge into Africa. As the British and their roads, railways and trading systems made their way inland the Gujaratis were part of a huge Indian workforce that went with them. Relatives of those already established in East Africa moved from Gujarat and a process of chain migration across the Indian Ocean began. During the 1970s it was these migrants who were forced by newly-independent African states to leave their homes and businesses and, as British passport holders, many made their way to Britain. Here they joined others who, having forged relationships with Britain and the British in Gujarat itself, had made the journey directly from India.

The Bangladeshi highlands seem an unlikely place to have a close relationship with the sea. However Sylhet and the nearby mountains of Assam are ideal places for growing tea, and became the hub of the huge tea growing industry in British India. To enable the export of the tea, steamships made their way up the navigable Kushiyara River to Sylhet. They needed stokers to fuel their boilers with coal, a demand that was met by local men. From Sylhet these men made their way downriver to Calcutta, Bombay's great sister port on the eastern end of the GT Road. As experienced stokers, the Sylhetis were well placed to get jobs on British ships that sailed all over the world, and which brought them to Britain.

A similar process was happening westwards. The waterways of the great Indus River system provided navigable routes which linked the GT Road with the ports of the Indian Ocean. However, the timber needed to build boats large enough for trade up and down the rivers could only be found in the mountains to the north. Massive cedar trees were floated down the rivers to the plains and Chach, the region where the GT Road crosses the Indus River at Attock, became a great centre for boat-building. Likewise Mirpur, where the River Poonch flows into the River Jhelum just north of the GT Road. Those who built the boats went on to crew them, and thus Chach and Mirpur developed a tradition of providing both the boats and the sailors that facilitated trade up and down these rivers.

This commerce prospered for centuries prior to the arrival of the British, but once they gained control of the region they built railways from the coastal cities of Bombay and Karachi to Lahore, Peshawar and beyond. By the 1870s goods could be transported much more quickly and cheaply by rail than by boat and the river-based trade rapidly declined. As the boatmen of Chach and Mirpur lost their jobs they journeyed south on the GT Road towards the booming port of Bombay. Here they worked in the docks, and then discovered the work that really broadened their horizons. Britain's merchant fleet was changing from sail to steam, and shovelling coal into the furnaces of coal-fired steamships was the hardest, dirtiest and most uncomfortable job available. It was also the hottest; engine-room temperatures in the tropics could reach 140° fahrenheit. Establishing a reputation for being tough and hard-working, ex-boatmen from Mirpur and Chach, along with the Sylhetis, soon gained a virtual monopoly as engine-room stokers on British ships leaving India. When these stokers returned home, some as 'sirings' or informal recruiting agents, they'd persuade others from their villages to follow them. Despite the working conditions, there were many volunteers as the jobs offered good wages compared with the money available locally. Those villages where many men became seamen – such as Wesa and Ghorghushti in Chach, Chakswari and Dudial in Mirpur – soon acquired a reputation for wealth that they retain to this day.

Joining the army was another option for those seeking escape from poverty. As described earlier, men would join the British Indian Army at recruiting stations along the GT Road, and after the 'Indian Mutiny' or 'Great Rising' of 1857 this recruitment was restricted to those who had fought on the side of the British. No recruitment took place east of Delhi, whereas the cantonments along the GT Road in the Punjab and North-West Frontier continued to recruit heavily from those Sikhs, Punjabis and Pathans who had helped the British quell the rebellion. Traditions of service developed within families. Regiments were built around a network of personal loyalties and it was these respected units from places like Jalandhar, Jhelum, Rawalpindi and Peshawar which went on to see active service overseas.

Alongside a few former sailors and the ayahs (nannies) and servants of British families returning from India, a small number of professionals – mainly doctors, businessmen or lawyers – established themselves in Britain from the mid-19th century onwards. However, it was the major conflicts of the 20th century that had the most profound effect on migration from the subcontinent to Britain. In 1914 Britain declared war on Germany on behalf of the entire British Empire. Over 130,000 of the 1.3 million Indians who made up the volunteer forces during World War I fought in France and Belgium, where over 8,000 of them were killed. Some veterans of this conflict went on to settle in Britain, many of them survivors drawn from the 12,000 wounded Indian troops, who were sent for treatment to the army hospital established in the Royal Pavilion in Brighton. Most of them eked out a living as pedlars, and between the wars could be found living in small groups, often with ex-seamen, in British seaports.

During World War II the Indian Army constituted the largest volunteer force in the world. Men signed up to fight rather than be conscripted and by 1945 the Indian Army was 2.5 million strong. As before, most of these men were recruited through established networks along the GT Road. The majority spent the war fighting in Asia, others were deployed to North Africa and Europe. Indians, particularly from Mirpur and Chach, were also critical to the manning of Britain's wartime merchant fleet. Indian seamen, previously protected from sailing on northern Atlantic voyages in winter, were 'released' from this restriction as the route became Britain's lifeline to North America. Many served on ships sunk on this and other routes. Due to a shortage of new vessels, some of those who were rescued were then redeployed to munitions work, for example in the engineering works of the West Midlands and the textile mills of northern England. When peace was declared in 1945 some stayed on in their new homes, and formed the nucleus of communities that grew with the arrival of de-mobbed soldiers and sailors. Stokers were also losing their jobs as coal-fired ships were replaced with those burning oil, and many looked for shore-based work in British ports or joined their compatriots in industrial areas inland.

The Partition of India in 1947 also brought a new set of problems for sailors from Mirpur and Chach. To travel from their homes in newly created Pakistan meant crossing a disputed frontier into India, where they were often treated with animosity. Travelling to and fro between their homes and Britain by working as seamen was difficult, and some made the decision to jump ship in British ports and seek land-based employment.

When the demand for labour emerged in Britain after World War II, it was these pioneers who sent word back to their family and fellow villagers of the opportunities available. They also sent remittances to families they had left behind. The money was accompanied by tempting, but often embellished, accounts of life in Britain. Those who returned home, either on a visit or to be replaced by another male relative, arrived bearing gifts and seemed by local standards to be very wealthy. These returnees often glossed over the long hours of hard and unpleasant work, often on the night shift. Negative accounts of poor housing and difficult living conditions in a cold climate were few, and were largely ignored and quickly forgotten.

Those who were comfortable in newly independent India and Pakistan did not want to come to labour in British factories. The vast majority of those who emigrated were poor, but who had the means to raise the fare to Britain. Some sold a plot of land, others pooled resources to send a young man. The very poor could not afford the journey. Along those stretches of the GT Road where property and farms all belonged to wealthy landowners, the landless workers may have been aware of opportunities available overseas, but were simply too poor

to take advantage of them. Many who had been displaced by Partition also took the view that having already lost their ancestral homes they had little to lose by selling any new property allocated to them and seeking better opportunities overseas.

Thus the process of chain migration developed a dynamic of its own throughout the 1950s where small groups of pioneers, originally from towns and villages along the GT Road, were joined by a large number of family, friends and neighbours. This was given an added impetus in the early 1960s for two reasons. Tighter immigration laws made it harder for people from overseas to live in Britain, or to travel back and forth to work. Most Asians were still groups of single men, often living in group houses, who thought of themselves as transients rather than settlers. Forced to make a decision many sent for their families to join them, and shortly before the enforcement of the Commonwealth Immigrants Act of 1962 many travelled to 'beat the ban'. The second reason was the building of the Mangla Dam in Mirpur. This huge project was designed to regulate the supply of water to the Pakistani Punjab and provide hydro-electric power to the rest of the country. Locally it displaced over 100,000 people who lost their homes, their land and their livelihoods. Although new towns were built around the edge of the huge reservoir, most say that the spirit of their former homes was lost along with the best farmland. Small amounts of compensation were paid by the Pakistani government and many used this money to join relatives already in Britain. It is estimated that 75% of the Pakistani population in Britain is of Mirpuri origin.

This process has changed not only the lives of the migrants themselves but also the places where they have settled. Often extended networks of family, and of towns and villages along the GT Road, have been re-established in the neigh-

right: India Gate in Delhi is inscribed with the names of over 100,000 Indian soldiers who died fighting on behalf of the British in World War I and in the North West Frontier during the First Afghan War of 1919.

bourhoods of British towns and cities. Ties with the homeland are not lost, but maintained by visits to family, by marriages and by investment in land, property and businesses. On a journey up the GT Road you will pass buildings bearing names such as London Tailors, Richmond Photo Studio, the Vindsor Palace Marriage Parlour and Wakefield Shoes. A similar journey along a typical British street of Asian-owned businesses name-checks the former homes of their proprietors: Dina Stores, Mangla Price Check, Khyber Palace Restaurant and the Ambala Sweet Centre. A huge variety of British regional accents can also be heard up and down the GT Road; from up-market shopping malls to dusty village streets where shop owners stock up on breakfast cereals and bottled water for the annual summer invasion of 'the Brits'.

The strength of links can also be measured by the number of travel agents, banks and businesses making goods for well-known British companies. Other concerns sometimes simply borrow a name for marketing reasons: British Biscuits, Topman Tailors and Vimpi's Burger Bar all attract those back from the UK as well as local people. Some have invested money made in Britain in community enterprises such as schools, health centres and places of worship. Palatial houses dot the towns and countryside, yet many remain empty as their owners live overseas. First generation migrants saw their move abroad as temporary, with retirement 'back home' their ultimate aim. Although people of all ages return for extended periods, the number of permanent returnees is relatively small. With families reunited in Britain, people do not want to leave children and grandchildren, undergoing the pain of separation for a second time. Since 1945, both Britain and the GT Road have been transformed by the process of migration and settlement, and will remain linked by it for many generations to come.

left: Grand houses built with remittances from Britain in Saleh Khana near Peshawar. The hills in the background are where the British Army established themselves, a strategic position now occupied by the radio masts of the Pakistani Army. Before World War II many local men joined the British Army, and subsequently travelled all over the world as members of the armed forces.
right: The streets of many towns and villages such as Saleh Khana are populated by women, children and the elderly as so many men have emigrated to Britain; most of those from Saleh Khana are now living in Dudley near Birmingham.

MOHAMMED SAEED AKHTAR, THE FOUNDER OF AKHTAR PHOTOGRAPHIC STUDIOS IN OLD MIRPUR TOWN, TELLS THE STORY OF HIS BUSINESS BEFORE IT WAS SUBMERGED BY THE BUILDING OF THE MANGLA DAM AND RESERVOIR. NOWADAYS PEOPLE CAN VISIT THE RUINS OF THEIR FORMER HOMES DURING THE DRY SEASON, WHEN TOWNS SUCH AS OLD MIRPUR AND DUDIAL (SEEN OPPOSITE) EMERGE FROM THE RECEDING WATER.

When I started in 1952, people used to have pictures done for pleasure only. Very few people at that time went to England. It was when they announced plans for the dam and the outcry that followed that the government said they would send people to England. You needed Rs.6000 for the passport and ticket. There were some travel agents that got people over to England. One of them left 120 notes each of Rs.100 by mistake in my shop. He turned up later in a bad way and I told him I had his money inside. He wanted me to have a reward but I refused. I told him to send me his men to have pictures taken – I needed clients. Mirpur had no electricity then. I tell you he rounded up so many people, it was like herds of sheep turning up to my place! I used to make Rs.150 to Rs.200 regular at a time when we paid less than Rs.2 for a kilo of meat!

My studio was right in the centre of the bazaar. It used to be the biggest photo studio in whole of Azad Kashmir and I built it myself – with a huge showroom and darkroom. I also had a shirt, an old tie and a coat in my studio as props. If they were already wearing a shirt, I put on the tie, the coat over the top and took the photo. I thought if these people are going for a passport, then their photo should make them look well dressed. That coat I used for fifteen years! It was in tatters but the lapel area still looked fine so I carried on using it! Then women started to come to me. So I kept a colourful dupatta at my studio and a chintz kameez. My customers would turn up wearing white and I used to explain that you didn't get good pictures in white, and I lent them this shirt and the dupatta. Women would put on the shirt on top of what they had on. Then I had flyers printed when electricity arrived in Mirpur, and in my adverts I said

my photos were taken with the help of electricity – even though they weren't. But that helped my business take off in a big way. Once I put on them, "Before leaving for England, get your quality passport photo at Akhtar Photographers – it will get you there!"

One night ten men turned up to my house at midnight – ten men! At midnight! Demanding they wanted photos there and then. I told them that was impossible and they threatened to drag me over to my studio, so I thought I'd better go with them! They'd seen some agent who'd promised to get them to England and asked them to bring him pictures without delay. That was the kind of urgency with which people set off for England, you know.

People couldn't believe the rush at my shop. Many people wanted to be my trainees because it was big business, and they thought they could cash in as well – and many of them did! It was nothing for me to get through one hundred men in a day. They came in their tens, having just gone to see an agent in a big group, they'd then come to me. I had twenty chairs all lined up in my studio for my customers but there was never anywhere to sit! Permanent queue! My friends would encourage me to go to England as well – I mean, they were all going themselves – and I used to say, "My England is right here. I have no need to go there." I was earning double sitting right here.

MEN FROM BIRMINGHAM EXAMINE THE FOUNDATIONS OF THEIR FORMER HOMES ON A VISIT TO THE VILLAGE OF KHARAK WHICH EMERGES FROM THE MANGLA DAM RESERVOIR DURING THE DRY SEASON. 90% OF THE PAKISTANI COMMUNITY IN BIRMINGHAM ARE OF MIRPURI ORIGIN AND ABDUL MAJEED MALLICK, WHO LIVED IN BRITAIN FOR MANY YEARS, RELATES THE EMOTIONAL TRAUMA OF MIGRATION FROM MIRPUR.

We used to live in the valley, in Dudial, which was surrounded by two rivers. On the north western side was the River Jhelum and on the eastern side River Poonch was flowing. They are still flowing. Whenever somebody left for abroad, his family and friends accompanied him to see him off up to the river. That was the point of departure you see – separation. So I accompanied my father in 1945 up to the River Poonch, then he crossed the river by boat. All the time he was looking behind, I was looking at him, both of us in tears. We never knew when we were going to see each other again because Second World War was going on. He was working in merchant navy, and all merchant navy ships were victims of German and Japanese gun boats. So knowing all these things, you can imagine when you depart from your father, what type of emotions you have – you can't express it in words. I remember I kept on weeping for the whole night and my mother was consoling me. Being the eldest son, many times I wished my father should have been here in the family, particularly on Eid festivals when all members sit together and celebrate. Every time we remembered him and every time we wished that he should have been in the family. So this torture of separation was realised every time by every member of the family.

The ship by which he was employed was sunk by Germans, then he boarded another ship, A D France. That ship was also sunk by German gun boats. He was saved and boarded another ship which took him to London where he had friends who took him to Birmingham. He wrote to us that I have decided that I must now stay and earn more money for the family. He was working in Newton Foundry. In those days most of our people were working as labourers in the foundries, textile mills, woollen mills, in railway and various departments. In those days the level of remittances was very high. He would write a letter that he has sent money, and this money order would take say 20 days to a month to travel from Birmingham to our village. Then we had banks over here, so the money was sent by draft. My father was paid very heavily in that foundry. He was very healthy and smart and very tall, and other labourers were getting £5 per week and he was getting £7. And when he worked overtime, then of course he was getting more. So my father invited other relatives – my uncle, then my two cousins, and a large number of our family then went to England, and most of them are settled in Birmingham. Total number of immigrants from my family must be 135 or so, because they have taken their families along now as well.

Old people are very keen to come back. They come and they build houses with this hope that their children will settle in Mirpur but my own experience and knowledge is that they are wrong. They were born here so they think this is their homeland, and home is always sweet home, so this is their sentiment. But when their children are born in Bradford or Birmingham, then they belong to that land, they are born there. So the disparity of hopes and thinking is this between parents and children – that parents want that they should come back to this area but children say, "No, England's my country, I can't stay here. You were born here, you live here, but I am going!" So there is a tussle between parents and children and it is a big problem.

CHOUDHRY MOHAMMED ALAM, OWNER OF LONDON TRAVEL SERVICE IN THE NEW TOWN OF MIRPUR, RELATES HOW HE SENT THOUSANDS OF MEN TO BRITAIN DURING THE 1950s AND 1960s.

I worked as a very ordinary sort of travel agent back then. There were agents who had thousands and thousands of customers. I did it as a sideline because I already had a full time job. I used to take a day or two off work maybe once a month, and accompany three or four men that I knew, and do their paperwork. The contract was Rs 6,000 and you made Rs 1,000 out of each case for yourself. So it was a good sideline. You got the passport made from Karachi, and the airport was then in Karachi also. It took 24 hours by rail to Karachi from Jhelum (nearest rail station to Mirpur), and then the return as well. I must have sent hundreds to England over the years.

You can't imagine how much these people were in love with the idea of going to England. That was their dream! You won't believe this – when they introduced the visa, then we couldn't send grown ups easily. Children could go easily though so some young men would say to me, "Send me as a child." Now, when they reached the airport a man would look them over, you know close-up, to make sure they didn't have stubble. Now, can you imagine how much it must hurt when you have your beard plucked out – each hair one by one! It's very painful. For the sake of being able to go to England, these men would have their long beards plucked out, so they could get away with looking like a young lad. One young lad I saw – he tied a scarf around his eyes because the pain was making his eyes water, and the barber was refusing to pluck the beard because he could see how it hurt. But the young lad persisted. They couldn't

shave you see – the stubble grows back the day after. Plucking gave a smooth finish you see. That's what they were willing to do!

I remember this funny story from 1962. There was a shepherd from our village who dreamed of going to England and I told him that for Rs 6,000 he too could go. That man sold all his sheep and goats and land to raise the money for his ticket. He was dreaming that he'd sell everything and go to England, and earn enough money to be able to buy back all his land and more besides! So I took him to Karachi and I remember we had such trouble finding boots for him. At the time, boots and a suit were the agent's responsibility before putting the passenger on the plane. We hunted all round Karachi and I was so worried. We found a pair in a shop window and they were so big around the toe that I told him to put some paper in to make them more comfortable. We used to pay Rs 300 to the police at the airport so our men wouldn't have any difficulties. Fitting, we called it. 'Have you been fitted?' meaning 'Have you done the bargaining?' All us agents would go on the roof of the airport until we were certain all our customers had been cleared by the police and were on the plane. I saw that three had been cleared but the one with the big boots I couldn't see. They'd stopped him because he was shuffling suspiciously in his boots! He'd never ever worn boots before you see.

left: Plots of land prepared for crops in Mirpur. With a growing population in rural areas such as this, the size of plots shrink with each succeeding generation. above: Visitors from Bradford relaxing in the roti house on the main street of Wesa. This town is one of the main centres of migration from the Chach region near Attock.

PAINTING A SHIP ON THE SIDE OF A VEHICLE IN A TRUCK PAINTING WORKSHOP IN DINA. IN THE STORY BELOW MOHAMMAD AYUB KHAN DESCRIBES THE IMPORTANCE OF THE SEA TO COMMUNITIES LIVING IN THE CHACH DISTRICT OF PAKISTAN.

Before Pakistan became independent, Bombay was the big port, or Calcutta. That's where all the big ships sailed from. There were quite a few people from Ghurghushtie [in Chach near Attock] that were already living in Bombay – this is before even the Second World War. They had businesses there like restaurants and that. These businessmen had their families still in Ghurghushtie so they would return to the village and everyone would come to know from their stories what a land of opportunity Bombay was. They told people that there was work available in Bombay. In my village there was really nothing to do besides farming, nothing else. People had very small landholdings so they could only grow enough for themselves. There wasn't much left to sell. I would say the whole of the Chach area was getting by like this. So you had to leave for a big city or get work on the ships if you wanted to save some money. That's how the interest grew you see. People saw these men that returned from Bombay every two or three years, and they thought, "I want to be like that. I want to earn the sort of money they earn, improve my living standard." They were suited and had good shoes. And they smoked cigarettes while the village folk were smoking hukkas!

My father was a farmer and he couldn't make ends meet so he thought he would try his luck as a seaman during the Second World War. Actually his friend suggested he should go to Bombay. He was a siring actually, that's like the head of the seamen. You can say he was a recruiter and he was looking for people to work on a merchant navy ship. The captain would tell him whenever he needed more people. Then he would come back to the village to take more people. He could only take people he knew, people he could trust, reliable ones. The recruiter was answerable to the captain, wasn't he! He had to give guarantee that these people will do the work. So as long

as you were strong and young, you could go – no other qualification. There were seven or eight sirings that were taking people from our area. They were putting coal in the furnace or doing the cooking work on board the steamships. All the workers were Indian and mostly Muslims, except for the captain and people like that; they were English, of course.

People were reluctant to work on ships so the recruiter had to try hard to persuade people. It was war times and ships got attacked all the time, so you had to be pretty desperate. I wouldn't say it's because Ghurghushtie people are especially brave. I think they had no choice. It was so dangerous that the steamships travelled in convoy because if one ship got attacked, the others might be able to rescue people. They were trade ships carrying food stuff or whatever to sell somewhere else but war affects everyone, doesn't it. And one day the ship in front got bombed and my father thought his ship would go down with it, but he was safe.

In the 1950s I reckon most people that came from Chach came on ships and came illegally – you know they jumped ship. To be honest it didn't really matter whether you were legal or illegal, because they were crying out for labour. I went with my dad to Tilbury Docks to meet this man from our village who was working on a ship that was docked there. We had a meal and then they set off back to Bradford with us! And when they got to Bradford, they sort of disappeared! They knew the ship was hardly going to hang around for them, so who was going to come after them? It was so normal those days. Anyone that went to meet a relative or a friend off a ship would end up leaving with them!

A man and his son on holiday from Bradford at the family home in Wesa near Attock.

above: Three young men from Woking, who are visiting Pakistan for a family wedding, stop for a meal on the GT Road in Jhelum.

right: Rickshaw driver and his vehicle outside the Glassy Junction, a bar on the GT Road in Jalandhar. The bar is named after the famous Glassy Junction in Southall, said to be the only pub in Britain to accept payment in Indian rupees.

above: Young men 'playing Holi' on the streets of Delhi. Holi is the Hindu festival of colours which celebrates the coming of spring. right: Young Delhi socialites dancing under a huge water fountain at a Holi celebration. Many of them are NRIs (non-resident Indians) who return on holiday to celebrate during the Holi party season.

भारत चाट भण्डार आगरा वाले

भारत चाट भण्डार

टिक्की, गोल गप्पे, भल्ले पापड़ी
शादियों व पार्टियों के लिए विशेष प्रबन्ध है। प्रो राजकुमार शर्मा

left: Shop keepers on the main street through Saleh Khana stock up on bottled water in preparation for the arrival of 'the Brits' during the school holidays. above: Street food on sale in Panipat.

above: Kharri Sharif is a well known shrine popular with visitors to Mirpur. Its graveyard contains the graves of some early migrants who died in Britain and whose bodies have been flown to Pakistan for burial in their 'home soil'. right: Mosque in new Dudial built with remittances from Britain.

Panja Sahib is one of the most important Sikh shrines built on the site where Sikhs believe that Guru Nanak, founder of the Sikh religion, performed various miracles.

Panja Sahib is now in Pakistan and lacks a local community to maintain it. Money for its upkeep comes from Sikhs living all over the world whose contributions are marked by marble plaques set in the floor around the temple.

left: A young groom from Walsall arrives at the house of his Mirpuri bride, and is greeted by her family. above: Once he is fed and garlanded he waits for the ceremony to begin.

left: At the conclusion of a village wedding in Pakistan, a *doli* was traditionally used to carry the bride from her own home to that of the groom and his family. Here she is carried to a waiting car at the beginning of a long journey to her married life in Britain.

right: The Golden Temple at Amritsar, the holiest of all Sikh shrines. Consecrated in 1604, the original temple was destroyed by Afghan invaders in 1761, and then restored by Maharaja Ranjit Singh during the 19th century.

above: A newly married bride and groom on the roof of the Golden Temple in Amritsar. right: Visitors to the Golden Temple at Amritsar pause for prayers in front of plaques commemorating Sikh military regiments.

left: The large and opulent homes of NRIs (non-resident Indians) in a village near Jalandhar. The water tanks on the roofs are designed to reflect the interests of the owners, and the presence of a plane signifies someone who has travelled overseas. above: Talvara is one of many villages in Mirpur that is virtually empty due to migration, and where most doors are found padlocked.

above: Labourer planting crops on the land of a Sikh family who divide their time between their businesses in both Jalandhar and the UK. right: Harbajan Singh, a former resident of Northern Ireland, delivering milk near Jalandhar. Most of those who work on his farm are from Bihar. Migration from the Punjab has set up internal movements within India itself; many move to this relatively wealthy area which is short of manpower for menial work.

Roadside hoardings in Peshawar.

A young man from Bradford hanging out in his trainers with local friends at the bicycle shop in Wesa.

above: The main street in Wesa. right: Making roti the traditional way at the home of a family who divide their time between the UK and India.

above: Street scene in the kite bazaar in Muridke. Kite making is an important home based industry in this town on the GT Road near Lahore. right: A man enjoying a drink at a roadside stall in the cinema district of Lahore.

left: The Star Art Studio in Ludhiana produces paintings of idealised Punjabi and British scenes. The former are mainly for export to expatriates in the UK, and the latter for those wanting to decorate their homes in India. above: Doorman at a themed restaurant in New Delhi.

A pilgrim in Amritsar rests next to an advert featuring Bollywood film stars.

I called my shop London Tailors because so many of our people live there. They come here and they have their daughters' dowries made up, all the embroidery and stitching, and jewellery to take back. I know you can get everything ready made there but you can't beat handmade. My shop's been here since 1978 and people see the name of my shop and then they come in. People assume that I've been to London and my work will be up to that sort of standard, and that's what I want people to think. I try not to disappoint my customers. I wouldn't want them to think I just came up with this name to impress them. I've got customers all over England, mainly in Bradford. Then there are a lot in Sheffield and Newcastle. You can say I'm their household tailor.

Industry and commerce have always been found along the GT Road, and in this age of globalisation, the horizons have simply expanded.

This shop in Mirpur is typical of many businesses which display names with British links, either as a reference to their owner's ties overseas or as a source of kudos for the goods and services they provide.

left: A truck painting workshop on the GT Road in Dina. above: The driver's cab of a rickshaw in Attock. The interiors of commercial vehicles are as elaborately decorated as their exteriors.

above: Sorting cotton at the Kohinoor Textile Mills in Rawalpindi. right: Finishing carpets at Raj Overseas, a firm in Panipat which manufactures for many international household names including Next and Laura Ashley.

Of course when the textiles business is shutting down in England it is coming to Pakistan, to India, to China. Pakistan has definitely benefited from the closure of mills in England. It's a blessing in disguise. Labour in England is very costly so their industry is shutting down. The businessmen of Britain and the manufacturers of Pakistan, both are benefiting out of this. We are gaining in terms of more business and they are gaining in terms of lower purchase price.

left: Afghani boys weaving carpets in Peshawar. They eat and sleep in the space next to the loom where they work. During the freezing winters, they migrate from the mountains of Afghanistan to Pakistan and return home during the warmer summer months.
right: Transporting yarn in Ludhiana, which claims to be the centre of India's textile industry.

We have been repairing knives since the time of Alexander the Great. When his convoy passed through Wazirabad, they stopped here at a small village to repair their swords and knives. Alexander the Great learnt that there are craftsmen here who know how to repair swords and things. So then they started making the swords and things here. This is the history in the books. So this is the profession of our forefathers. I am third generation in cutlery. Although it is a cottage industry in Wazirabad, this is the capital of cutlery. This is a mini Sheffield.

left: Making Raleigh bikes for export at Hero Cycles in Ludhiana, the largest bicycle factory in the world. It produces over 18,000 bikes on an average day, and many British firms have now moved their manufacturing to the site.
right: Grinding cutlery in one of the thousands of such workshops in Wazirabad. Much of it is made for export, including a large proportion of the Asian catering industry in the UK.

If you're carrying perishables – you know grapes, tomatoes, green chillies – then you drive non stop for 36 hours at a time! I've done that! I've driven for 48 hours non stop. Two nights and two days! Without sleep! You just have to keep yourself awake. You have to take something obviously – you name it, opium, ganga, cannabis, tobacco, anything goes! You try staying awake and driving like that! And you eat two chapattis instead of four – a full stomach makes you sleepy. You have to keep stopping at trucker hotels and pouring water over yourself to stay awake. There are truckers who only ever carry perishables so this is how they live. You see it's good money. You get incentives. They tell you "you'll get an extra 2,000 rupees if you get the truck there within 24 hours." So every hour is crucial when you are carrying perishables. And if you don't get there on time, then you lose out on your wages because your load isn't saleable! Everyone wants to carry perishables – that's where the money is!

left: Sikh taxi drivers with their fleet of Ambassador cars. Manufactured in India since 1958 the car remains little changed from the original model whose design was based on the Morris Oxford manufactured in Britain.
right: Trucker's cafe at Taxila.

above: Truck stop near Gujrat in Pakistan. right: An unfinished flyover in Ludhiana.

ACKNOWLEDGEMENTS

IN INDIA: Col Malhotra (Retd) & General Shankar Prasad (Retd) at the Gymkhana Club in Delhi; Prarit Agarwall at the Radisson Hotel in Jalandhar; Sandeep Kang; Paramjit Kaur; Sanjeev Singh Guram; Serbjeet Kaur Guram; Gurmeet Rai; Anita Roy at Oxford University Press; Gurbaksh Kaur Baga Sufi Sant; Nirupama Sekhi; Kashmira Singh and staff at the British Council in Delhi.

IN PAKISTAN: Dr Yasmin Raashid; Hussain Jafri & Zulfiqar Nabi Malik of Millennium Tours; Major Ayaz of the Khyber Rifles; Minoo Bhandara at the Murree Brewery; Sardar Adnan; Dr Ejaz Khan; Safdar Nawab Khan; Canon Huw Thomas at Edwardes College in Peshawar; staff at the British Council in both Islamabad and Peshawar.

IN ENGLAND: Mumtaz Sultana Khan; Derek Smith; Isma Almas; Kryssy Fordham; Elizabeth Smith; Alexei Smith; Mushtaq Ahmed; Ajay Chhabra; Rajinder Paul Johar; Roger Ballard; Steve McClarence; Rozina Visram; Camilla Adler-Jenson; Mark Suggitt, Michael Callaghan, Maggie Pedley, Pav Chana and the staff of Bradford Industrial Museum; Kate Chatfield, Dr Nick Mansfield and staff at The People's History Museum in Manchester; Bridget Izod, Anne Brown and Jane Heap at Bradford Libraries.

This book was developed from an exhibition first commissioned and shown by Bradford Industrial Museum and the People's History Museum in Manchester. It is part of a project supported by a grant from the 'Their Past Your Future' programme which received funding from the Big Lottery Fund and was managed and delivered by the Museums, Libraries and Archives Council. The programme offered funding to explore innovative and creative ways of increasing community learning and young people's knowledge and understanding of the impact and contemporary significance of conflict.